P9-DWB-783

THE DONKEYS' TALES

Dedication

This book is dedicated to grandparents and grandchildren
everywhere and the stories that bind them together.

It is especially for Clay, Tyler, Sarah, Will, and Andy.

Author's Note

One morning while reading my Bible, it struck me that the Scriptures mention a donkey
as part of two events in Jesus' life: the donkey present at the time of His birth and the donkey
He rode into Jerusalem on Palm Sunday. *What if* those two donkeys were related?
The answer to that question is this story.

Although *The Donkeys' Tales* is based on Scriptural narrative, I do not intend it to be taken as fact.

Adele Bibb Colvin

Adele Bibb Colvin

Birmingham, Alabama

1998

Text copyright © 1998 by Adele Bibb Colvin
Illustrations copyright © 1998 by Peyton Hamilton Carmichael
Book design by Alice Pederson

First published by Crane Hill Publishers, 1998
Published by arrangement with the author by
         Pelican Publishing Company, Inc., 2008

First printing, 1998
First Pelican edition, 2008

Library of Congress Cataloging-in-Publication Data

Colvin, Adele Bibb, 1940–
The story of Jesus as told in the donkeys' tales/by Adele Bibb Colvin; illustrated by
Peyton Hamilton Carmichael.
p.   cm.
Summary: A retelling of selected events from the life of Christ based on biblical accounts and presented from
the point of view of the donkeys present at the time.
ISBN-13: 978-1-58980-627-6
1. Jesus Christ—Biography—Juvenile literature. [1. Jesus Christ—Biography.]
I. Carmichael, Peyton Hamilton, 1940–   ill. II. Title.
BT302.C65   1998
232.9'01—dc21
[b]   97-30495
                                        CIP
                                        AC

Printed in Singapore

Published by Pelican Publishing Company, Inc.
1000 Burmaster Street, Gretna, Louisiana 70053

The Story of Jesus as Told in

THE DONKEYS' TALES

by Adele Bibb Colvin   Illustrated by Peyton Hamilton Carmichael

PELICAN PUBLISHING COMPANY

GRETNA 2008

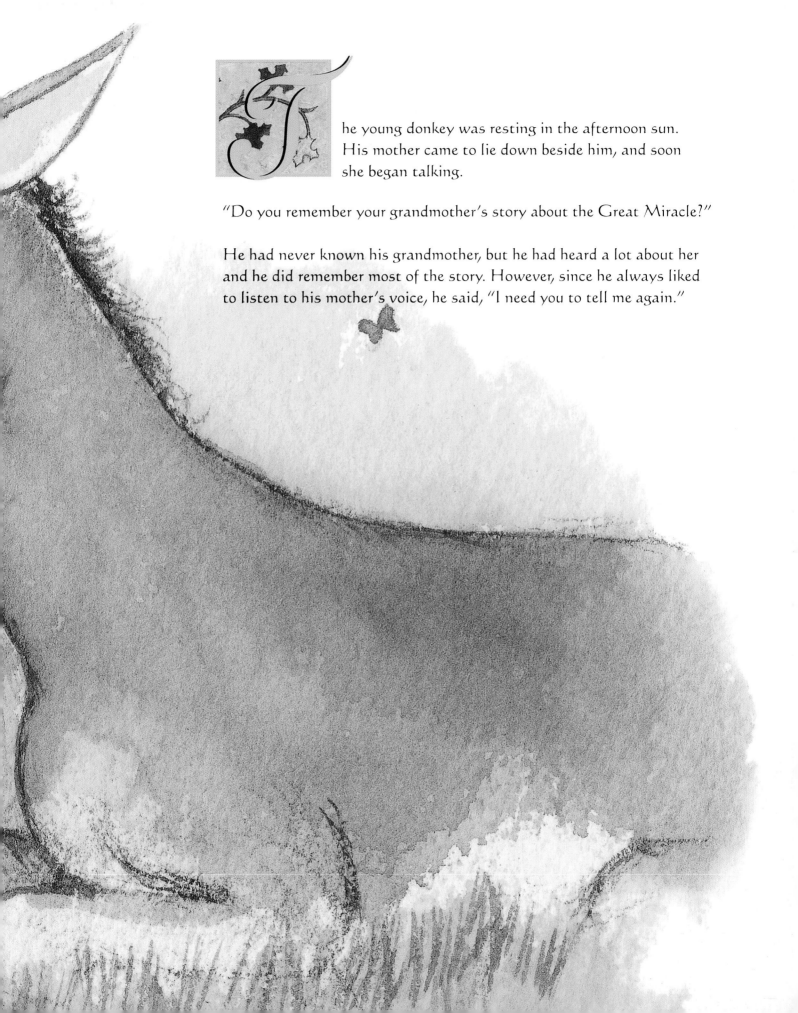

he young donkey was resting in the afternoon sun. His mother came to lie down beside him, and soon she began talking.

"Do you remember your grandmother's story about the Great Miracle?"

He had never known his grandmother, but he had heard a lot about her and he did remember most of the story. However, since he always liked to listen to his mother's voice, he said, "I need you to tell me again."

"Well," she said, "it began because her family, who lived in Nazareth, had to make a journey to the city of Bethlehem to register for a census and pay taxes to the Roman government. It was not such a good time to go because Mary was about to have her first baby. Joseph, her husband, packed everything he thought they would need and tied the bundles on your grandmother's back, leaving room for Mary. 'I'll try to make this trip as easy as I can for you,' he told her.

"They traveled along rough, dusty roads and finally arrived in Bethlehem only to find that there was no place to sleep. At last, one innkeeper offered space in his stable. Your grandmother was very happy to be able to rest, but she was especially happy that she would be in the same room with her family.

"As they were getting settled, Mary told Joseph that her baby would be born quite soon. Suddenly there was the most wonderful music sounding throughout the heavens, and warm light streaming from a very bright star shone through the small window of the stable!

"Your grandmother knew something special must be happening but did not immediately realize that it was happening right there in the stable, to her own family!"

"Later that night, shepherds came asking to see the baby about whom the angels had sung, declaring that He would be found lying in a manger in Bethlehem. 'We were told,' said the shepherds, 'that this Child is the Savior, Christ the Lord.'

" 'Why, they are talking about Jesus, Mary's baby!' she exclaimed to herself. Your grandmother stood gazing in awe at everyone there and wondering, 'How could I have been the one donkey in all the world to have this honor?' She knew that she would need to be extra careful and protective of Mary and this special baby when they were able to go home. As she fell asleep that night, she sang softly to herself."

Lo, the holy light. See the star.
Hear the angels sing
The glories of this night of all nights.
All hail the Infant King.

See the mother there, robed in light,
holding her baby so dear.
She sings to him and the angels hear
a song that echoes their own.

See the father there, kneeling in prayer,
gazing on the Child,
Who was giv'n this night by God above
to him and to Mary so mild.

See the shepherds there, standing in awe,
called to the stable so bare,
To come and see God's wondrous sight
on this most holy night.

"In the coming days, there were more visitors, some *Wise Men* (perhaps they were even kings) from far away. They, too, had seen the magnificent star and followed its light to the stable in Bethlehem, bringing gifts to honor Baby Jesus."

See the Wise Men there, from afar,
drawn on this journey of faith,
To find their King come down to
earth and celebrate His birth.

"But they also brought some bad news: King Herod, a mean and jealous man, had heard rumors about a baby who would be King and wanted the Wise Men to report back to him when they found this baby. However, Wise Men are just that—*wise*. They knew they should not tell Herod anything, and so after celebrating Jesus' birth with Joseph and Mary, they took a different road home.

"Just when your grandmother thought that they also would be going home, an angel appeared to Joseph and told him to take Jesus and Mary to Egypt because they were in danger from King Herod."

Hear the angel's voice,
bringing God's word:
There is danger here,
So flee with Jesus to Egypt's land,
away from Herod's hand.

"Well, off they went on another journey. Naturally, your grandmother was anxious about her new responsibility; she had to keep the Holy Child and His mother comfortable and safe.

"After the first few days, Joseph was able to relax a bit since it then seemed certain that they were not being followed by Herod's soldiers.

"The route was a hard one, most of it through hilly desert wilderness, and Mary was worried about keeping her newborn son outside for so long. She wrapped His clothing and blankets in ways that would shield His tender skin from the hot sun and dry winds.

"Jesus was generally a very good baby, but at those times when He was unhappy and crying, your grandmother tried to keep her gait steady and rhythmic in an effort to rock Him to sleep."

"The days were long and the barren land seemed so endless that my mother told me she had even begun to wonder if there really was such a place as Egypt! But, of course, there was, and they did get there.

"They had been in Egypt for about two years when the angel came once more to Joseph, this time saying that Herod had died and they should return to the land of Israel."

Hear the angel now, with a new command:
Herod's gone so it's safe
To take the Child back to Israel
and live in Holy Land.

"All of them were so happy with this news that the prospect of another long trip through the desert didn't even seem too bad. Your grandmother was no longer nervous about her task, but she continued to be very careful with her special passengers.

"Certainly, Mary was not a problem, but Jesus had become an active and inquisitive little boy who liked to run along the trail and explore things. Your grandmother had to keep her eye on Him *every moment* lest He stray too far or fall and hurt himself."

"She said she breathed a great sigh of relief when they were back in Israel and had settled once more in the city of Nazareth.

"Joseph was again a carpenter, and a few years later I was born. When Jesus was not helping Joseph in the shop, He and I spent many happy hours together. Throughout my childhood, my mother often sang her song to me and told about the night of Jesus' birth and the many adventures she had while traveling with her family."

"My goodness! I nearly forgot to mention the incident that scared us very badly. It was the year that Jesus was twelve and our whole family went to the annual Passover Feast in Jerusalem. After the holiday, we were a full day into our journey home when we discovered that Jesus was missing! My mother was particularly upset. Even though she was very old, she still considered Him her special charge and felt that somehow she had not been watchful enough.

"We quickly turned around, anxiously searching for Him among the crowds of people who were also leaving the festival. We got all the way back to Jerusalem before we finally found Him talking with teachers in the Temple. Everyone was puzzled by the answer He gave when Mary and Joseph asked why He had stayed behind: 'Did you not know I must be in my Father's house?' However, the one important thing to us was finding Him safe.

"This time when we left for Nazareth, your grandmother decided she would just walk beside Jesus every step of the way."

The little donkey loved the story, but he was always somewhat jealous when he heard it. "If only I had been born sooner," he thought, "maybe I could have been the one to carry them instead. Then *I* would be the one in all the stories."

Time passed, and after the little donkey grew up, he went to live with a family near the village of Bethany. One day while he was tied to a tree near their house, two men came and loosened the rope. He had never seen them before, and he was frightened. His owners saw what was happening and ran over.

"This is *our* donkey," they said. "What are you doing?"

The men answered, "The Lord has need of it," and they turned to walk away, taking the animal with them.

The young donkey was still afraid. He had never really been away from his house except to pull a threshing board in his family's nearby wheat fields or to help carry wood for fires. "What's happening? What are they going to do to me?" Questions filled his head as he reluctantly went with the two strangers and as his home and his family vanished from sight.

Soon they came to a place called the Mount of Olives where a small group of people were gathered, talking excitedly of a trip into Jerusalem. The two men stopped, put their cloaks over the donkey's back, and lifted a man to sit on him. Since he had never been ridden before, he tried to shake the rider off—but before he could, the man spoke softly to him and gently stroked his neck.

They began to move, following the two men who had
untied him from the tree. Soon many, many people lined
the road, shouting "Hosanna" and waving palm leaves.
They seemed to want to see and touch and talk to the man
who sat on his back. "Who *is* he?" he kept wondering.

Suddenly, some in the crowd began calling out, "Jesus!
Jesus!"

"Could it be?" the young donkey asked himself. "Could it
be that this *man* Jesus is my grandmother's *baby* Jesus all
grown up?" With each step, as the procession to Jerusalem
continued, he became certain in his heart that this man
was indeed Christ the Lord whom his grandmother had so
lovingly carried long ago. Now he, too, was most blessed
among all the donkeys in the world.

As he walked carefully along with his Holy Passenger,
he added a new verse to his grandmother's song and said to himself,
"Grandmother, wherever you are, I hope you can see us!
I'm taking good care of Him for you."

See the people there, crowding the way, hailing Jesus the King

As He travels to Jerusalem on this triumphant day.

The Donkeys' Tales

By Adele Colvin © 1996

Lo,   the   ho - - ly   light.   See_____   the   star.
See   the   mo - - ther there,   robed_____   in   light,
See   the   fa - - ther   there,   kneel - ing in   prayer,
See   the   shep - - herds there,   stand - ing in   awe,
See   the   Wise___ Men there,   from___   a - far,
Hear   the   an - - gel's voice   bring - ing God's word:
Hear   the   an - - gel   now   with a new com - mand:
See   the   peo - - ple   there,   crowd - ing the   way,

Hear   the   an - - gels   sing   the   glo - ries of_____   this
holding her   ba - - by so   dear.   She   sings   to   Him and the
ga - - zing on_____ the   Child   who was giv'n this night____ by
called to the sta - ble so   bare,   to   come   and see____ God's
drawn on this jour - ney of   faith   to   find   their King____ come
There   is   dan - - ger   here,   so   flee   with Je - sus to
Her - rod's gone so   it's   safe   to   take   the   Child back to
hail - ing Je - sus the   King   as He tra - vels to_____ Jer -

night of   all   nights____ all   hail   the   In - - fant   King.
an - - gels hear____ a   song   that   ech - oes their   own.
God____ a - - bove____ to   him   and to Ma - ry so   mild.
won - - drous sight____ on   this   most   ho - - ly   night.
down   to   earth____ and   cel - e - brate____ His   birth.
E - - gypt's land____ a   way   from   Her - - rod's   hand.
Is - - ra - el____ and   live   in   Ho - - ly   Land.
u - - sa - lem____ on   this   tri - umph - - ant   day.

✱ high notes for last verse only